Thoughts From the Sea of My Mind

A collection of inspired and inspirational poems

By

Gordon D. Mahon

Copyright © 2011 by Gordon Demetrius Mahon

All Rights Reserved

Published

By

Diaspora Vibes Publishing, LLC

ISBN-13: 978-0615500430

Dedication

To Janet, Gian, Giorgio and Gabriel

My Mother Carol

and

My Family

About the author

Gordon D. Mahon is a songwriter/poet who lives with his family in a suburb of Orlando. He is also an accomplished Aerospace Engineer. Gordon developed a deep passion for music growing up in Brooklyn and from frequent visits to relatives in Trinidad & Tobago. The pictures in the book were taken by the author from various trips to Trinidad & Tobago, Oahu and St. Thomas USVI.

Contents

Acknowledgements	i
Breathe	1
Diaspora Vibes	5
Bliss	10
Eternal	14
As Time Passes By	18
Everyday	22
Go to Sleep	26
The End is Near	30
Thank You God for This Gift	34
This is Just the Beginning	38

Acknowledgements

There are many souls who have had a significant impact on my life. Everyone is my teacher. Some teachers I wish to thank are: Grey, Wendell Langford, Victor Ezell, Fr. Joseph Nugent, Fr. Caleb Buchanan, Michael Urmeneta, Sister Jenna and Dr. Jerel Eaglin.

Thus far the journey has been amazing! Most importantly, I am grateful to God, my mother and to my world - Janet, Gian, Giorgio and Gabriel - my unending sources of inspiration!

Breathe

Sometimes you are like a bomb
Simplest thing sets you off
Was it the red wire or the blue?
Just don't know what to do.

People can trip if they want
The truth is it's not about you
No matter what they say or do
Truly it is not about you.

Breathe and be still
You can, you have the will
Reclaim your inner peace
The storm has ceased.

Here they come, thoughts of judgment:
"Do it this way", "Say it like this"
Why must this be?
Why am I so cruel to me?

Breathe and be still
You can, you have the will
Reclaim your inner peace
The storm has ceased.

I feel trapped, I feel helpless
What can I do to be free?
I will stop, I will breathe
I will learn to love me.

Breathe and be still
You can, you have the will
Reclaim your inner peace
The storm has ceased.

People can trip if they want
The truth is it's not about you
No matter what they say or do
Truly it is not about you.

Breathe and be still
You can, you have the will

Reclaim your inner peace
The storm has ceased.

What can I do to be free?
I will stop, I will breathe
I will learn to love me
I will learn to love me
I will learn to love me
I will learn to love me
I will learn to love me
I will learn to love me
I will learn to love me.

Diaspora Vibes

Children of the Diaspora
We are one, of the same tree
Let us remember
So we may be free.

Dispersed by the winds we were
We face today with no fear
We have the Ancients' wisdom today
Let's use it to forge our way.

Diaspora Vibes, Diaspora Vibes
We are the Vibes of the Diaspora
Feel our rhythm, feel our beat
Feel the love, feel the heat.

Our destiny is in our hands
We can change the way we think
Let us create positive plans
With the Ancients' wisdom we must link.

Diaspora Vibes, Diaspora Vibes
We are the Vibes of the Diaspora
Feel our rhythm, feel our beat
Feel the love, feel the heat.
(Repeat)

It's the mindset we use
To greet those we meet

It's the mentality that guides our feet
I choose the person I will be
I choose the person I will be.

Diaspora Vibes, Diaspora Vibes
We are the Vibes of the Diaspora
Feel our rhythm, feel our beat
Feel the love, feel the heat.

Children of the Diaspora
We are of the same tree
Let us remember
So we may be free
We choose the people we will be
We choose the people we will be.

Diaspora Vibes, Diaspora Vibes
We are the Vibes of the Diaspora
Feel our rhythm, feel our beat
Feel the love, feel the heat.
(Repeat)

Children of the Diaspora
We are of the same tree
Let us remember
So we may be free
We choose the people we will be
We choose the people we will be.

Diaspora Vibes, Diaspora Vibes
We are the Vibes of the Diaspora
Feel our rhythm, feel our beat
Feel the love, feel the heat.
(Repeat)

Bliss

Where are you?
Where do I find you?
Looking down at my shoe
Where? Oh where do I go?

Are you here, there, where?
Chasing windmills
Not under the chair
Not above the tree
Where could you be?

My bliss, my bliss
What is this, what is this?
My bliss, my bliss
Where is this, where is this?

My bliss, my bliss
Ah, but of course
There you are

Where you always have been
All I had to do was look within.

Time spent, years go by
Now and then, hints fly
Time to focus
Too much in my hands
Amazin' how this stuff expands.

My bliss, my bliss
Ah, but of course
There you are
Where you always have been
All I had to do was look within.

My bliss, my bliss
Ah, but of course
There you are
Where you always have been
All I had to do was look within.

I am free now
I have walked out of the
Cave into the dawn
Between many things no longer torn
There is peace, and within that power.

My bliss, my bliss
Ah, but of course
There you are
Where you always have been
All I had to do was look within.

Eternal

Why do you do the things you do
Mental assault, Physical assault
I thought you knew
It is all for naught
I cannot be destroyed.

You continue on your path
Does this make you feel powerful?
Putting me under your wrath
Are you possibly full?
I cannot be destroyed.

I am an eternal soul
I am powerful
Don't you see my friend?
I cannot be brought to an end.

Perhaps you should redirect your energy
I am sure you can find

Something besides me
All of this must have you annoyed
As I said, I cannot be destroyed.

I am an eternal soul
I am powerful
Don't you see my friend?
I cannot be brought to an end.

Why do you do the things you do
Mental assault, Physical assault
I thought you knew
It is all for naught
I cannot be destroyed.

I am an eternal soul
I am powerful
Don't you see my friend?
I cannot be brought to an end.

I am an eternal soul
I am powerful

Don't you see my friend?
I cannot be brought to an end.

Perhaps you should redirect your energy
I am sure you can find
Something besides me
All of this must have you annoyed
As I said, I cannot be destroyed.

I am an eternal soul
I am powerful
Don't you see my friend?
I cannot be brought to an end.

As Time Passes By

In the beginning
Your contributions
I did not appreciate
Your wisdom
I did not take.

Your brilliance
I was blinded to
By my own illusions
Round and round
The insanity widens.

As time passes by
I realize more and more
The gift you are to my life
Reality of your blessedness
Grows deeper and deeper.

The road can be hard

We make it difficult for ourselves
Patience is necessary
And what helps
Is knowing you're here with me.

As time passes by
I realize more and more
The gift you are to my life
Reality of your blessedness
Grows deeper and deeper.

Get rid of these shackles
They are of no use
Free now to see
Everything and
All that you are to me.

As time passes by
I realize more and more
The gift you are to my life
Reality of your blessedness
Grows deeper and deeper.

As time passes by
I realize more and more
The gift you are to my life
Reality of your blessedness
Grows deeper and deeper.

Get rid of these shackles
They are of no use
Free now to see
Everything and
All that you are to me.

As time passes by
I realize more and more
The gift you are to my life
Reality of your blessedness
Grows deeper and deeper.
(Repeat)

Everyday

Everyday, Everyday
I rise higher and higher
Leaving behind what I thought
I could not transcend.
To this there will be no end.

Another sunrise.
A new way of thinking.
An awakening.
A new friend.
Passing what was the end.

Everyday I am given
Is another day You bless me.
Each day I see new mercies from You.
Each day another grace comes through.

I start the day with a prayer.
Beginning with a need.

Finally it's answered perfectly.
Answered perfectly.

Everyday I am given
Is another day You bless me.
Each day I see new mercies from You.
Each day another grace comes through.

Everyday I am given
Is another day You bless me.
Each day I see new mercies from You.
Each day another grace comes through.

There is no doubt
It is clear in my soul
Not carrying the troubles of ole
It is here in front of me
Just need the eyes to see.

Everyday I am given
Is another day You bless me.
Each day I see new mercies from You.

Each day another grace comes through.

There is no doubt
It is clear in my soul
Not carrying the troubles of ole
It is here in front of me
Just need the eyes to see.

Everyday I am given
Is another day You bless me.
Each day I see new mercies from You.
Each day another grace comes through.
(Repeat)

Go to Sleep

There he goes again
Ah, didn't I just feed him!
There goes that familiar din.

You know I will always be here for you.
There is so much I want to
Teach and show you.

But now it is time for sleep.
Go to sleep.
Go to sleep.
I need my rest too
So I can take care of you.

Groggy in the head.
Stumbling out of bed.
Either hungry or wet.
Don't know yet.

I will take you to Trinidad.
I will take you to Jamaica.
All for you to know your culture.
Bake and Shark on Maracas Bay.
Blue sea and bright sun all day.

But now it is time for sleep.
Go to sleep.
Go to sleep.
Go to sleep.
Go to sleep.
I need my rest too
So I can be strong to care for you.

He is teaching me patience
If it is not one thing it must be the other
What a precious countenance!

You are my heart
I love you so
I will be here wherever you go.

But now it is time for sleep.
Go to sleep.
Go to sleep.
I need my rest too
So I can take care of you.

But now it is time for sleep.
Go to sleep.
Go to sleep.
I need my rest too
So I can take care of you.

The End is Near

It seems I have been in this rut for a time
I am still weary of being a mime
But was it really a waste with all I gained
Going through the motions to the end of the day.

How much longer must I endure this situation?
It takes so much effort to defeat the frustration
I cannot wait to move on from here
So lightness will be what I wear.

The end is near
I can feel it
I can see it
It is here
My freedom will be sweeter.

I feel trapped in this strife
A prisoner in my own life
An illusion wrapped tightly

Onto my mind which is free.

The end is near
I can feel it
I can see it
It is here
My freedom will be sweeter.
(Repeat)

I know I am in control
I am working towards my goal
There is a sense of peace
My effort will not cease.

The end is near
I can feel it
I can see it
It is here
My freedom will be sweeter.
(Repeat)

It seems I have been in this rut for a time
I am still weary of being a mime
But was it really a waste with all I gained
Going through the motions to the end of the day.

I know I am in control
I am working towards my goal
There is a sense of peace
My effort will not cease.

The end is near
I can feel it
I can see it
It is here
My freedom will be sweeter.
(Repeat)

Thank You God for This Gift

Thank you God for this gift
I am sitting on the floor
Watching you play with a belt
And I am in bliss
So thankful for you and your presence.

Thank you God for this gift
I am so grateful
My love will preserve
So precious a gift
I promise I will serve.

I could not be happier
You are so wonderful
You are rolling around
I tickle your tummy
Your laugh, it is so funny.

Thank you God for this gift

I am so grateful
My love will preserve
So precious a gift
I promise I will serve.

Playing in the other room
You scurry across
The floor to me
Don't want to be left alone
Just want to be home.

Thank you God for this gift
I am so grateful
My love will preserve
So precious a gift
I promise I will serve.

You come up to me
Place your smooth
hand on me
How I melt when you do this
The joy I feel

The joy I feel.

Thank you God for this gift
I am so grateful
My love will preserve
So precious a gift
I promise I will serve.

This is Just the Beginning

In from the cold, out with the old
Awake from the sleep, in from the deep
I made some wrong choices
Thought I was right
Just trying to cope
Did not see any sign of hope.

Livin' in my head, awake from the dead
In denial, every day's no longer a trial
What was I thinkin'?
Could only see the flaws
Dark night of the soul
What do I use to fill the hole?

This is just the beginning baby
Romance you till you scream with delight
There will be no end in sight
To this joy, this love
I promise you

This is just the beginning.

Wonderful, take everything personal
Ping-pong anyone? Games not done
Always in this endless cycle
Get me outta here!
Come to a realization
This is not fun.

This is just the beginning baby
Romance you till you scream with delight
There will be no end in sight
To this joy, this love
I promise you
This is just the beginning.
(Repeat)

www.ingramcontent.com/pod-product-compliance
Lightning Source LLC
Chambersburg PA
CBHW041812040426
42450CB00001B/12